Counting Bats

by Elizabeth Sch

SCHOLASTIC INC.

Photographs © 2012: iStockphoto: 8 (Kevin Smith), 1 (Valeriy Kirsanov); Minden Pictures/Kim Taylor: cover; Photo Researchers/Merlin Tuttle/BCI: 5; Superstock, Inc.: 4 (age fotostock), 2 (F1 ONLINE), 6 bottom (imagebroker.net), 3, 7 bottom, 7 top (Minden Pictures), 6 top, 6 center (Robert Harding Picture Library).

No part of this publication may be reproduced, stored in a retrieval system, or transmitted in any form or by any means, electronic, mechanical, photocopying, recording, or otherwise, without written permission of the publisher. For information regarding permission, write to Scholastic Inc., Attention: Permissions Department, 557 Broadway, New York, NY 10012.

ISBN 978-0-545-49723-7

Cover and interior designed by BHG Graphic Design. Photo research by Liza Charlesworth.

Copyright © 2012 by Lefty's Editorial Services. All rights reserved. Published by Scholastic Inc.
SCHOLASTIC, GUIDED SCIENCE READERS, and associated logos are trademarks and/or registered trademarks of Scholastic Inc.

12 11   19/0

Printed in China.   68

I see one bat.

I see two bats.

I see three bats.

I see four bats.

I see five bats.

1, 2, 3, 4, 5!

I see lots and lots of bats!